Kid Pick!

Title: _____

Author: _____

Picked by: _____

Why I love this book: _____

_____

_____

_____

SEP 1 3 2004

ROCKFORD PUBLIC LIBRARY

Rockford, Illinois

http:www.rpl.rockford.org

DEMCO

EXTREME SURVIVAL
POLAR REGIONS

Sally Morgan

Raintree
Chicago, Illinois

EXTREME FACTS

Look for the penguin in boxes like this.
Here you will find extra facts, stories,
and information about the polar regions.

Editorial Manager: Joyce Bentley
Project Editor: Lionel Bender
Text Editor: Clare Hibbert
Design and Make-up: Ben White
Picture Research: Cathy Stastny
Production: Kim Richardson
Consultant: John Stidworthy

Library of Congress Cataloging-in-Publication Data:
Morgan, Sally.
Polar regions / Sally Morgan.
v. cm. -- (Extreme survival)
Includes bibliographical references (p.   ).
Contents: What are polar regions? -- The year round -- Under the ice -- Polar plants -- Arctic wildlife -- Arctic migrants -- Antarctic wildlife Arctic peoples -- People on the move -- Working on ice -- Keeping warm -- Ice facts -- Ice words -- Ice projects.
ISBN 1-4109-0003-7 (lib. bdg. : hardcover) -- ISBN 1-4109-0362-1 (pbk.)
1. Polar regions--Juvenile literature. [1. Polar regions. 2. Ecology.] I. Title. II. Series.
QH84.1.M67 2003
577.5'86--dc21   2003005200

Acknowledgments
We wish to thank the following individuals and organizations for their help and assistance and for supplying material in their collections:
CORBIS Corporation/Images: pages 1, 3, 9 centre, 15 bottom (James L. Amos/CORBIS), 27, 28, 29. Ecoscene: pages 9 bottom (Kjell Sandved), 23 bottom (Robert Weight), 24 (Graham Neden). Oxford Scientific Films Photo Library: pages 2 and 6/7 top (Ben Osborne), 8 (Colin Monteath), 10 (Konrad Wothe), 11 top (Martyn Chillmaid), 11 bottom (Niall Benvie), 13 top (Owen Newman), 13 bottom (Tom Ulrich), 14 bottom (Daniel Cox), 16 bottom and 17 top(Doug Allan), 17 bottom (Tui de Roy), 19 bottom (Doug Allan), 20 (Richard and Julia Kemp/SAL), 22 (Colin Monteath), 23 top (Bruce Herrod), 25 top (Doug Allan), 25 bottom (Kim Westerskov), 26 (Colin Monteath/Hedgehog House), 31 (Doug Allan). PhotoDisc Inc.: pages 4 top (Sami Sarkis), 15 top (Robert Glusic), 19 top (Philippe Colombi), 30 (Neil Beer). Still Pictures: pages 5 (B & C Alexander), 7 middle (Fritz Polking), 12 (Alain Pons), 18 bottom (B & C Alexander), 21 left (Pal Hermansen), 21 right (Hans Hvide Bang). Cover photos: Front, Oxford Scientific Films Photo Library (Colin Monteath), Back, CORBIS Corporation Diagrams and maps: Stefan Chabluk.

CONTENTS

▼ A killer whale swims in search of prey (see page 9).

ICY EXTREMES

Earth has two polar regions. The Arctic is an ice-covered ocean found at the North Pole. The Antarctic is a huge icy continent at the South Pole. These regions are unlike any other on Earth, covered by ice and snow, with extreme climates.

The animals and plants of the polar regions live in one of the toughest environments on Earth. The winters are long and dark. The temperatures fall far below freezing, 32°F (0°C). It can be so cold that water spilled from a bucket freezes before it hits the ground.

▲ In spring, blocks of ice break off the polar ice sheets and then slowly melt.

Antarctic

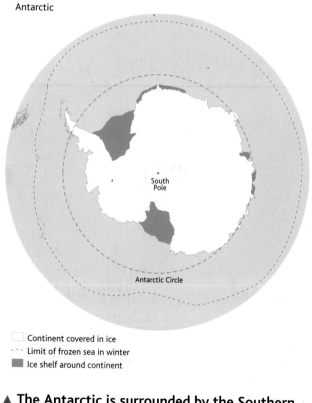

South Pole

Antarctic Circle

☐ Continent covered in ice
- ⌐ Limit of frozen sea in winter
■ Ice shelf around continent

Arctic

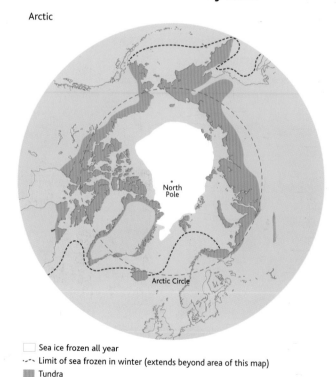

North Pole

Arctic Circle

☐ Sea ice frozen all year
- ⌐ Limit of sea frozen in winter (extends beyond area of this map)
■ Tundra

▲ The Antarctic is surrounded by the Southern Ocean. During the Antarctic winter, the ocean ice reaches for hundreds of miles beyond the continent—as shown by the red line.

▲ The Arctic is an ocean that is surrounded by land. The central part of the Arctic Ocean is frozen all year, but in winter the ocean ice reaches as far as the land—the green areas.

In the polar regions, strong winds make it feel even colder. In summer the days are long, but the temperature can still be below freezing. Not surprisingly, only a few animals, and even fewer plants, can survive in these conditions.

Living in the polar regions is hard for people, too. People have lived in and around the Arctic for thousands of years. They have learned to live with the extreme cold. In contrast, the Antarctic was unknown to people until the first explorers reached it during the 1800s. Even today, there are no permanent inhabitants, just visiting scientists and tourists.

ANTARCTIC ICE

Antarctica is the highest, coldest, and windiest continent in the world. It is larger than the United States, Mexico, and Europe combined. Its ice sheet contains 70 percent of the world's fresh water.

▼ Although ice floes—small sheets of ice—appear fragile, they can support a person or a polar bear.

THE YEAR ROUND

During a polar summer there is nonstop daylight. At the North Pole, the sun rises above the horizon on March 21 and stays above it until September 22. It then stays set until the following March. So during the winter there is little light, just a faint glow.

It is the same at the South Pole, except at opposite times. When it is summer at the North Pole, it is winter at the South Pole. The Antarctic is much colder than the Arctic. The average winter temperature is about -76°F (−60°C). The ocean freezes over at a rate of 2.5 miles (4 kilometers) each day. By midwinter, the ocean ice doubles the area of the Antarctic ice. The extreme cold means that the animals and plants found in the Antarctic are different than those in the Arctic.

▼ As Earth circles the Sun, for half of the year the Arctic tilts away from the Sun, pictured here. Then the Antarctic tilts away.

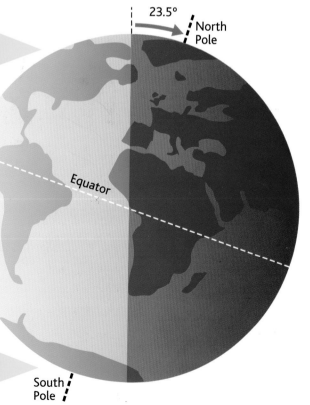

Sun's rays at Pole

▶ Earth's axis—the imaginary line around which the planet spins—is tilted at an angle to the Sun. With the Arctic tilted away, it is the northern winter.

Sun's rays at Equator

▶ The Sun's rays have to travel furthest to reach the polar regions, so their warming effect there is not as great as at the equator.

Sun's rays at Pole

23.5°

North Pole

Equator

South Pole

◀ Icebergs float like an ice cube in a drink. Only the tip of the iceberg rises above the surface of the sea. More than 80 percent of it lies underwater. In the Antarctic, icebergs often look pink. This is due to tiny plant-like algae that are buried in the ice.

▲ When the temperature rises, the pack ice breaks up into ice floes. Animals such as these Canadian walruses rest on the ice floes.

FROZEN IN THE GROUND

The Siberian salamander, a type of amphibian, can live in temperatures down to -58°F (−50°C). In Siberia, Russia, summer lasts only four months. For the rest of the year, the salamander survives below ground, hibernating at a temperature a little above freezing.

Although the climate is cold, the air is dry and there is little rainfall and snowfall. Fierce, cold winds suck away the moisture. The Arctic and the Antarctic are actually cold deserts. They are among the driest places on Earth.

LIFE IN POLAR SEAS

Even though the polar seas are frozen over for much of the year, they are rich in life. The blanket of ice protects the water underneath from the worst of the weather. The temperature of the water beneath the ice is just above freezing.

Few plants are found beneath the ice. Thick ice blocks out the light that plants need to survive and make food. Tiny plants do grow where the ice is thinner or where there is no ice at all. These plants are eaten by tiny sea creatures. Together the tiny plants and animals make up plankton, which is food for larger creatures, such as fish and whales.

▼ An Antarctic fishing catch. These icefish are predators—they hunt other creatures for food. They have huge jaws and sharp teeth to grip their prey.

Living on the ocean floor, below the ice, are animals such as anemones, worms, sea squirts, shrimp, and sea lice. These animals grow very slowly because the energy needed for growth is used for keeping warm instead. However, they live for a long time. There is a type of Antarctic limpet that can live for more than 100 years, while some sponges are known to be several hundred years old.

FISH ANTIFREEZE

The icefish has a liquid similar to antifreeze in its blood. Antifreeze is a liquid added to a car's radiator to stop the engine from freezing up in winter. In the icefish, the "antifreeze" stops the fish's body from freezing solid.

▲ Killer whales hunt other whales and seals. They swim through the pack ice as it is breaking up, and will even break through thin ice to grab unsuspecting prey moving on the ice.

▶ This small shrimplike animal—an Arctic amphipod—can survive temperatures a few degrees below freezing.

POLAR PLANTS

The Antarctic, because it is covered in ice, has only a few simple plants. Most of the Arctic plants are found in a habitat known as the tundra. This is the land between the frozen ocean and the northern forests. It is mostly lowlying, with very few trees.

In the tundra the ground is frozen to depths of up to 2,625 feet (800 meters). In summer, the warmth of the sun melts the top foot (30 centimeters) or so, but the meltwater cannot drain away. The wet, soggy ground is ideal for plants such as mosses, cotton grass, and sedge.

▼ The broad, round shape of this Canadian Arctic poppy plant means that, when snow falls, the weight of the snow will not damage the plant's stems.

TRACKING THE SUN

To make sure the maximum amount of light falls on their petals, some Arctic flowers follow the sun as it moves across the sky. The petals trap the heat and the extra warmth attracts insects that pollinate the flowers.

▲ There are no tall trees on the tundra. Instead there are dwarf trees like this willow in Iceland, that grow along the ground rather than up. The tasty leaves are eaten by caribou, musk oxen, and birds such as the ptarmigan.

Arctic plants have to be able to survive extremes—the long, cold winter followed by a short, warm summer. There is a constant wind, too, which removes moisture from leaves and stems. Many plants grow low to the ground or in the shelter of small rocks to keep out of the wind, and most have small leaves to cut down on water loss.

The growing season lasts only a few months. The plants have to grow new leaves and produce flowers and seeds within this time. The seeds lie in the frozen ground until the following year.

▲ The bilberry is a tough, low-growing shrub with small leaves. Its fruit is eaten by birds and mammals.

KEEPING WARM

Polar animals face the problem of keeping warm. Many move away when the weather becomes too cold. For those that stay behind, there is a constant struggle for survival.

Insects, fish, and many sea creatures have little control over their body temperature. If their environment is cold, their bodies are also cold. In very cold conditions, these animals hardly move. Many Arctic insects spend the winter at the bottom of frozen pools or buried in the soil.

Birds and mammals, however, keep their temperature the same, moving around to make warmth when temperatures drop. The body temperature of an Arctic fox stays about 102°F (39°C), even in conditions below freezing. A lot of energy is needed to keep warm, so polar birds and mammals have to eat plenty of food.

FAMILY LIFE

In December, the female polar bear gives birth to her cubs in an underground den in the snow. The family stays in the den until spring—then comes out to feed all summer long.

▲ The polar bear has a large body covered in thick fur and a layer of fat beneath its skin. This helps to keep the bear warm in cold weather.

Keeping in body heat is important. Polar bears and musk oxen have thick fur. Birds are covered in feathers. Seals, whales, and dolphins have a layer of fat called blubber beneath the skin. Thick fur, feathers, and blubber all stop heat from escaping. In fact many polar animals risk overheating if the temperature rises above freezing.

▲ The fur of the Arctic fox is excellent for keeping in heat. The fox can doze in the snow for an hour in temperatures as low as -58°F (-50°C) with no ill effects.

◀ The musk ox of Canada and Alaska has an outer layer of long hairs that reach to the ground. Beneath this is a thick layer of short, fine hairs.

ARCTIC SUMMER SURVIVAL

The warmer weather and plentiful food supply attract many large animals to the tundra for the short Arctic summer. They feed and breed on the tundra until the cold weather returns. Then some move into the shelter of the northern forests, while others travel further south.

Each spring caribou and reindeer travel to the tundra to feed and to give birth to their calves. The journey is dangerous. Even though they keep together in herds, the caribou are hunted by wolves. When the wolves come close, the frightened caribou start to run. Most of the animals can outrun the wolves, but not injured or very young caribou. It is often these animals that are attacked by the wolves.

MOSQUITO MENACE

In July the Arctic air is alive with swarms of mosquitoes and other biting insects. They have to feed on the blood of birds or mammals to survive and lay their eggs.

▼ The caribou have long, powerful legs that help them survive the treacherous journey to and from the tundra.

The boggy pools of northern Russia are almost lifeless by autumn. In the summer they are buzzing with flies and other insects. This attracts many birds, which feed on the insects.

The tundra provides plenty of plant food for lemmings, hares, and ground squirrels. These small mammals are hunted by predators, such as the Arctic fox, stoat, and snowy owl. These predators have growing young to feed. Some Arctic mammals, such as the stoat, can put off giving birth until conditions warm up. Survival depends on there being food for the newborn.

▼ Millions of geese, ducks, and swans flock to the Canadian tundra each spring to breed and raise their young. This early visitor is a snow goose.

ANTARCTIC WILDLIFE

The Antarctic is much colder than the Arctic, and there is no land route for animals to get to a warmer climate in winter. So Antarctic animals are all marine mammals and birds, dependent on the ocean for food. In winter some of these mammals head north to warmer waters, returning in the spring.

The most common birds are penguins, albatrosses, and petrels. Penguins cannot fly and are clumsy on land, but they are excellent swimmers. They have a torpedo-shaped body and use their wings like paddles. They dive to depths of more than 657 feet (200 meters) to catch fish and squid. Thick feathers and a layer of blubber keep them warm.

PENGUIN FATHER

It is the job of the male Emperor penguin to keep the egg warm. He huddles on the ice with all the other males for four months. He has to survive the freezing temperatures, strong winds, and winter darkness.

▶ These Emperor penguin chicks are two months old. They have fluffy, soft feathers that keep their bodies warm and act as a barrier to the wind.

Some seals can survive in the icy waters all year round. The Weddell seal dives down hundreds of feet for cod, squid, and shellfish. It has to come to the surface to breathe, and has strong front teeth to scrape open a breathing hole in the ice.

Like penguins, seals have an extra layer of body fat to keep them warm. They can also burn this fat for energy during periods when food is scarce. Hence, mother seals feed their cubs milk that is rich in fat.

▲ Leopard seals are fearsome hunters. They wait in the water for penguin chicks to take their first swim, then hunt them down.

▼ Skuas are birds that rob penguins of their eggs or chicks. They work in pairs—one skua pulls the adult penguin off its nest while the other steals the egg or chick.

ARCTIC PEOPLES

Today there are about two million people living inside the Arctic Circle, in Canada, Alaska, Iceland, Greenland, and Russia. The Inuit and Aleut have lived in the Canadian Arctic for thousands of years.

People living in the Arctic cannot grow crops, so they hunt seals, whales, birds, and fish for food. Their prey also provide them with clothing. Thick animal fur is ideal for keeping out the cold. Sealskin is used to make waterproof boots known as *mukluks* and hooded coats called *parkas*.

▼ The Inuit people catch ringed seals and fish through carved holes in the ice. The seals provide skin, meat, and fat (blubber) for cooking.

The lifestyles of both the Inuit and the Aleut are changing. The people are using modern ideas and new technology to help them survive in the Arctic. Their homes are built from the latest materials, which are excellent at keeping in the heat and keeping out the snow and wind.

Their diet has changed and there are more Western-style foods available. However, they still rely on animals for much of their food. Hunting is changing, too. The harpoons of the past have been replaced by modern hunting rifles. Getting around is easier. Inuit hunters used to travel by dog sled. Nowadays the most common form of transportation is the skidoo, or snow-bike.

▲ This Inuit village is on Baffin Island, Canada. Nowadays most Inuit live in modern houses like these. The windows have triple glazing to keep in the warmth.

IGLOOS
In the past, the Inuit people lived in igloos—homes made from ice. These domed-shaped houses are surprisingly warm. The ice is good at trapping the warmth from people's bodies and their fires.

◄ An Inuit stands beside an igloo that he has just built. He cut each block of packed snow from the ground and shaped them to fit together tightly.

PEOPLE ON THE MOVE

Many people who live in the Arctic keep herds of reindeer. These people are nomads. Instead of living in one place, they travel with their animals in search of new feeding grounds. Reindeer herders include the Nenets of Siberia, Russia, and the Sami.

The Sami live in an area called Lapland, which stretches across northern Russia, Finland, Sweden, and Norway. In winter the Sami shelter with their herds in the northern forests. Even there it is bitterly cold. In summer, they follow their herds hundreds of miles north to the tundra, well within the Arctic Circle.

▲ Nenets tribesmen use reindeer-drawn sleds to keep up with their herds. In the background of this tundra scene are isolated conifer trees.

The Sami and the Nenets depend on the reindeer for milk, meat, and skins to make clothing. While they are traveling with their herds, they live in reindeer-skin tents. They transport their belongings across the snow on reindeer-drawn sleds.

FINDING NORTH

A compass usually points to the north, but near the North Pole the needle just points toward the ground. Arctic peoples rely on the position of the stars in the sky to find their way instead.

▲ The Sami attract tourists, whom they welcome as a source of income. Tourists are often invited to share a meal with them in their tents.

Like the Inuit, the way of life of the Sami and the Nenets is changing. Some of the richer Sami who own many reindeer do not travel with their herds any more. They use helicopters and planes to move their families to the summer grounds, leaving a few people to travel with the herds.

▲ Traditional Sami clothes are colorful, with elaborate embroidery. The fur-lined hats, gloves, and boots keep out the cold.

DANGERS OF THE COLD

The Antarctic is normally too cold for people to survive there. Even in summer, temperatures are low enough to freeze your breath as it leaves your mouth.

The Antarctic does not belong to any nation, but people from many countries work there. They have to wear clothing that keeps the heat in and the extreme cold out. Usually they wear several layers, with waterproof jackets and pants. Every part of the body has to be covered. Even in these clothes, no one can stay outside for more than 30 minutes in the winter.

COLD COMA
Normal body temperature is 98.6°F (37°C). Below 95°F (35°C), the body stops working and goes into a lifeless state, or coma. This is called hypothermia. Without medical help, the person will die.

▼ In Antarctica, every part of the body—even the face—needs protection from the bitter cold. The husky has a thick coat to keep it warm.

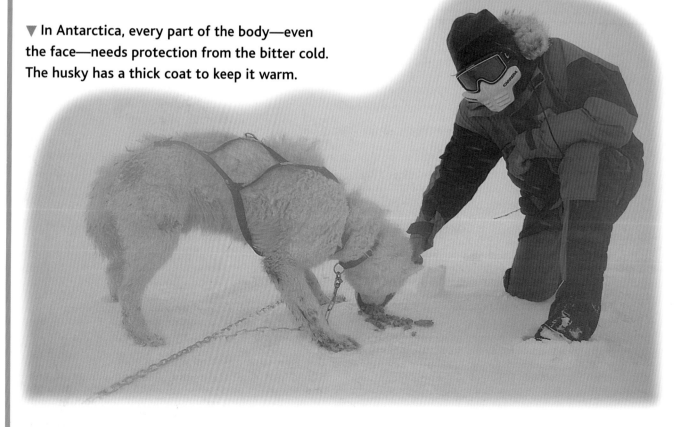

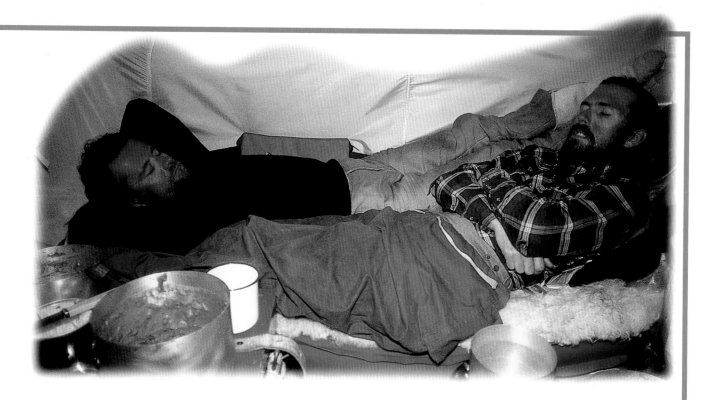

▲ These researchers are sheltered overnight in a tent. They have taken off their outer clothing so that it can dry.

Frostbite is a constant danger. This is when part of the body gets so cold that the flesh freezes. It affects the fingers, toes, ears, and nose first. The freezing causes terrible damage and people lose whole fingers and toes. Frostbite can be avoided by wearing the correct clothing and by taking off any wet clothing as soon as possible.

People burn up a lot of energy trying to keep warm in cold climates. So they eat foods that are rich in fat. Chocolate is an ideal food in the Antarctic as it is full of fat and is easy to store and carry.

▶ This scientist is dressed to combat the Antarctic weather. Thick-soled, fur-lined boots keep his feet warm.

ANTARCTIC BASES

Scientists working in Antarctica stay in specially built bases. These provide essential shelter from the weather. Without them people could not survive.

There are no trees in Antarctica, so all the building materials have to be shipped in. Most bases are a group of small huts. Some house scientific equipment. Others are lived in. The huts are basic but comfortable. Electricity comes from a generator stored in a separate hut.

▼ Research stations are built on legs so that the living areas are not buried by snow in winter. The United States, Russia, France, Britain, Chile, and Australia all have research stations on Antarctica.

RECORD LOW

The lowest temperature ever recorded in Antarctica is -124°F (–86.9°C). At that temperature, human flesh freezes in seconds, and the air is so cold that just breathing it in would damage your lungs.

Surprisingly, people in Antarctica fear fire more than the cold. The air is dry. One spark from the generator could start a fire, then the strong winds could spread it from hut to hut. That would be a disaster. Even if the scientists escaped the fire, without shelter the cold would kill them.

▲ Scientists use caterpillar-track vehicles like this Sno-Cat to transport equipment and supplies. The vehicles have antifreeze systems so moving parts do not seize up in the cold.

▶ Antarctic bases constantly monitor the weather. Here scientists are preparing weather-checking instruments to be carried by a balloon high into the atmosphere.

Most bases take precautions against fire and have fire patrols. Having separate huts means there is less chance of the whole base burning down. The scientists also place emergency food, fuel, tents, and a radio in a hut built well away from the rest. Even so, if a fire happened in winter there would be no chance of rescue before the spring.

POLAR REGIONS: FACTS

RACE TO THE POLE

On December 14, 1911, a group of Norwegians led by explorer Roald Amundsen became the first people to make the journey to the South Pole. They were closely followed by a British team lead by Captain Robert Scott. The Norwegian team used dogs to pull their sleds over the ice, making better time than the British, who were pulling their own sleds. Sadly, Scott and his team died on their way back.

WEDDELL SEAL

The only seal that breeds before the end of the Antarctic winter is the Weddell seal. The female breaks through a crack in the ice and climbs onto the ice sheet. She gives birth there, using her own body to shelter the newborn pup from the wind.

▼ This is a research base on Ross Ice Shelf in the Antarctic.

UNDERGROUND NESTS

Lemmings survive the Arctic winter by digging tunnels and living under the ground. They build nests of grass in the tunnels. Their body heat is enough to keep the temperature in the nest at about 50°F (10°C)—even if it is freezing above ground.

THE NORTHWEST PASSAGE

Many explorers lost their lives trying to seek the Northwest Passage, an ocean route through the Arctic that links the Atlantic and Pacific Oceans. The first person to make the journey was Robert McClure in the 1800s. Conditions were so bad that his ship was stuck in ice for two years. He finally completed his journey in 1854.

▲ This baby harp seal from Canada has a beautiful white fur coat that keeps it warm—but also attracts fur hunters.

RARE SEAL

The Ross seal is the rarest of the Antarctic seals. Its bulgy eyes help it to find fish and cuttlefish in the dark water beneath the ice.

A CHANGE OF COLOR

The ptarmigan is a bird that lives in the Arctic all year round. It has feather-covered legs for extra protection against the cold. In summer its feathers are gray-brown. In winter the bird grows white feathers so that it is harder for predators to spot against the snow.

POLAR REGIONS: SUMMARY

Polar regions present living things with extreme conditions ranging from temperatures far below freezing to strong winds and drought. Plants and animals have evolved a variety of ways to survive in this environment.

Most polar plants have stems and leaves that trap warmth and prevent loss of moisture. The plants are low-growing to avoid the chilling effects of the wind. Polar animals have thick fur, feathers, or blubber to keep warm. In winter some animals move to warmer climates. Others hibernate. People can survive at the poles only with special clothing and shelter, and on a diet of high-energy foods.

▼ Walruses live around the northern coasts of America, Europe, and Asia. They use their tusks to haul themselves onto ice floes and to smash breathing holes in the ice.

FURTHER INFORMATION

You can visit polar regions on the Internet. Here are some good places to start.

The Arctic Studies Center
http://www.mnh.si.edu/arctic/index.html
This site offers information about northern peoples and cultures, including the Inuit and Aleut.

Zoom School
http://www.EnchantedLearning.com/school/
   Antarctica/index.shtml
This site can tell you all about Antarctica, including surviving the cold, explorers, animals, and even dinosaurs and fossils of the region.

If you would like to read more about polar regions and the animals and people who live there, check out these books.

Butz, Christopher. *Tundra Animals*. **Chicago: Raintree, 2003.**
All about the variety of animals that live in the frozen wilderness.

Malcolm, Penny. *Polar Bear*. **Chicago: Raintree, 2000.**
Information about this fascinating animal, its life, and its habitat.

▲ The king penguin, like all penguins, feeds in the water. It often dives deep to hunt squid, but mostly eats fish that it catches near the surface.

GLOSSARY

This glossary explains some of the words used in this book that you might not have seen before.

Amphibian
type of animal that usually lives on land but breeds in water, such as a frog, toad, or salamander. Adult amphibians have four legs and a moist skin.

Antarctic/Arctic Circle
imaginary line marking the South/North Polar region

Blubber
thick layer of fat just under the skin. It helps keep in body heat.

Caribou
North American reindeer

Environment
natural surroundings

Frostbite
when body parts freeze. Unless frostbite is treated quickly, the flesh dies and has to be cut away.

Generator
machine used to produce electricity

Habitat
place where an animal or plant lives

Hibernating
going into a deep sleep, living on stored supplies of energy

Hypothermia
when a person's temperature drops too low for the body to function properly

Iceberg
enormous mass of ice, floating in the sea

Ice floe
sheets of ice, formed when the pack ice starts to break up

▼ Huskies are used to pull sleds in the Arctic and Antarctic. They can survive in temperatures of -40°F (–40°C).

Mammal

type of animal that has fur or hair. The female gives birth to live young, which she feeds with milk.

Meltwater

melted snow or ice

Nomad

one of a group of people who move from place to place with their animals to find food

Pack ice

big area of floating ice

Plankton

tiny plants and animals that float in water, often near the surface, and are carried by the currents

Pollinate

to transfer pollen to a flower to fertilize it and so make seeds

Predator

animal that hunts other animals—its prey—for food

Prey

animal that is hunted for food by a predator

Sled

vehicle on ski-like runners, usually pulled by dogs or reindeer. Sleds are used to carry loads or people over the snow.

Tundra

flat, treeless zone between the Arctic ice sheet and the northern forests where the soil below 1 foot (30 cm) deep is permanently frozen

▼ In the Arctic summer, the sun never sets—this is midnight and the sun is far above the horizon. Its warming rays have started to melt the ice floes.

INDEX